THE JPS B'NAI MITZVAH
TORAH COMMENTARY

Be-ḥukkotai (Leviticus 26:3–27:34)
Haftarah (Jeremiah 16:19–17:14)

Rabbi Jeffrey K. Salkin

T0334677

The Jewish Publication Society · Philadelphia
University of Nebraska Press · Lincoln

INTRODUCTION

News flash: the most important thing about becoming bar or bat mitzvah isn't the party. Nor is it the presents. Nor even being able to celebrate with your family and friends—as wonderful as those things are. Nor is it even standing before the congregation and reading the prayers of the liturgy—as important as that is.

No, the most important thing about becoming bar or bat mitzvah is sharing Torah with the congregation. And why is that? Because of all Jewish skills, that is the most important one.

Here is what is true about rites of passage: you can tell what a culture values by the tasks it asks its young people to perform on their way to maturity. In American culture, you become responsible for driving, responsible for voting, and yes, responsible for drinking responsibly.

In some cultures, the rite of passage toward maturity includes some kind of trial, or a test of strength. Sometimes, it is a kind of "outward bound" camping adventure. Among the Maasai tribe in Africa, it is traditional for a young person to hunt and kill a lion. In some Hispanic cultures, fifteen year-old girls celebrate the *quinceañera*, which marks their entrance into maturity.

What is Judaism's way of marking maturity? It combines both of these rites of passage: *responsibility* and *test*. You show that you are on your way to becoming a *responsible* Jewish adult through a public *test* of strength and knowledge—reading or chanting Torah, and then teaching it to the congregation.

This is the most important Jewish ritual mitzvah (commandment), and that is how you demonstrate that you are, truly, bar or bat mitzvah—old enough to be responsible for the mitzvot.

What Is Torah?

So, what exactly is the Torah? You probably know this already, but let's review.

The Torah (teaching) consists of "the five books of Moses," sometimes also called the *chumash* (from the Hebrew word *chameish,* which means "five"), or, sometimes, the Greek word Pentateuch (which means "the five teachings").

Here are the five books of the Torah, with their common names and their Hebrew names.

> ‣ **Genesis (The beginning), which in Hebrew is Bere'shit (from the first words—"When God began to create").** Bere'shit spans the years from Creation to Joseph's death in Egypt. Many of the Bible's best stories are in Genesis: the creation story itself; Adam and Eve in the Garden of Eden; Cain and Abel; Noah and the Flood; and the tales of the Patriarchs and Matriarchs, Abraham, Isaac, Jacob, Sarah, Rebekah, Rachel, and Leah. It also includes one of the greatest pieces of world literature, the story of Joseph, which is actually the oldest complete novel in history, comprising more than one-quarter of all Genesis.

> ‣ **Exodus (Getting out), which in Hebrew is Shemot (These are the names).** Exodus begins with the story of the Israelite slavery in Egypt. It then moves to the rise of Moses as a leader, and the Israelites' liberation from slavery. After the Israelites leave Egypt, they experience the miracle of the parting of the Sea of Reeds (or "Red Sea"); the giving of the Ten Commandments at Mount Sinai; the idolatry of the Golden Calf; and the design and construction of the Tabernacle and of the ark for the original tablets of the law, which our ancestors carried with them in the desert. Exodus also includes various ethical and civil laws, such as "You shall not wrong a stranger or oppress him, for you were strangers in the land of Egypt" (22:20).

> ‣ **Leviticus (about the Levites), or, in Hebrew, Va-yikra' (And God called).** It goes into great detail about the kinds of sacrifices that the ancient Israelites brought as offerings; the laws of ritual purity; the animals that were permitted and forbidden for eating (the beginnings of the tradition of kashrut, the Jewish dietary laws); the diagnosis of various skin diseases; the ethical laws of holiness; the ritual calendar of the Jewish year; and various agricultural laws concerning the treatment of the Land of Israel. Leviticus is basically the manual of ancient Judaism.

> ‣ **Numbers (because the book begins with the census of the Isra-elites), or, in Hebrew, Be-midbar (In the wilderness).** The book describes the forty years of wandering in the wilderness and the various rebellions against Moses. The constant theme: "Egypt wasn't so bad. Maybe we should go back." The greatest rebellion against Moses was the negative reports of the spies about the Land of Israel, which discouraged the Israelites from wanting to move forward into the land. For that reason, the "wilderness gen-eration" must die off before a new generation can come into ma-turity and finish the journey.

> ‣ **Deuteronomy (The repetition of the laws of the Torah), or, in Hebrew, Devarim (The words).** The final book of the Torah is, essentially, Moses's farewell address to the Israelites as they pre-pare to enter the Land of Israel. Here we find various laws that had been previously taught, though sometimes with different wording. Much of Deuteronomy contains laws that will be im-portant to the Israelites as they enter the Land of Israel—laws concerning the establishment of a monarchy and the ethics of warfare. Perhaps the most famous passage from Deuteronomy contains the *Shema,* the declaration of God's unity and unique-ness, and the *Ve-ahavta,* which follows it. Deuteronomy ends with the death of Moses on Mount Nebo as he looks across the Jordan Valley into the land that he will not enter.

Jews read the Torah in sequence—starting with Bere'shit right af-ter Simchat Torah in the autumn, and then finishing Devarim on the following Simchat Torah. Each Torah portion is called a parashah (di-vision; sometimes called a *sidrah,* a place in the order of the Torah reading). The stories go around in a full circle, reminding us that we can always gain more insights and more wisdom from the Torah. This means that if you don't "get" the meaning this year, don't worry—it will come around again.

And What Else? The Haftarah

We read or chant the Torah from the Torah scroll—the most sacred thing that a Jewish community has in its possession. The Torah is written without vowels, and the ability to read it and chant it is part of the challenge and the test.

But there is more to the synagogue reading. Every Torah reading has an accompanying haftarah reading. Haftarah means "conclusion," because there was once a time when the service actually ended with that reading. Some scholars believe that the reading of the haftarah originated at a time when non-Jewish authorities outlawed the reading of the Torah, and the Jews read the haftarah sections instead. In fact, in some synagogues, young people who become bar or bat mitzvah read very little Torah and instead read the entire haftarah portion.

The haftarah portion comes from the Nevi'im, the prophetic books, which are the second part of the Jewish Bible. It is either read or chanted from a Hebrew Bible, or maybe from a booklet or a photocopy.

The ancient sages chose the haftarah passages because their themes reminded them of the words or stories in the Torah text. Sometimes, they chose *haftarah* with special themes in honor of a festival or an upcoming festival.

Not all books in the prophetic section of the Hebrew Bible consist of prophecy. Several are historical. For example:

The book of Joshua tells the story of the conquest and settlement of Israel.

The book of Judges speaks of the period of early tribal rulers who would rise to power, usually for the purpose of uniting the tribes in war against their enemies. Some of these leaders are famous: Deborah, the great prophetess and military leader, and Samson, the biblical strong man.

The books of Samuel start with Samuel, the last judge, and then move to the creation of the Israelite monarchy under Saul and David (approximately 1000 BCE).

The books of Kings tell of the death of King David, the rise of King Solomon, and how the Israelite kingdom split into the Northern Kingdom of Israel and the Southern Kingdom of Judah (approximately 900 BCE).

And then there are the books of the prophets, those spokesmen for God whose words fired the Jewish conscience. Their names are immortal: Isaiah, Jeremiah, Ezekiel, Amos, Hosea, among others.

Someone once said: "There is no evidence of a biblical prophet ever being invited back a second time for dinner." Why? Because the prophets were tough. They had no patience for injustice, apathy, or hypocrisy. No one escaped their criticisms. Here's what they taught:

> God commands the Jews to behave decently toward one another. In fact, God cares more about basic ethics and decency than about ritual behavior.
> God chose the Jews *not* for special privileges, but for special duties to humanity.
> As bad as the Jews sometimes were, there was always the possibility that they would improve their behavior.
> As bad as things might be now, it will not always be that way. Someday, there will be universal justice and peace. Human history is moving forward toward an ultimate conclusion that some call the Messianic Age: a time of universal peace and prosperity for the Jewish people and for all the people of the world.

Your Mission—To Teach Torah to the Congregation

On the day when you become bar or bat mitzvah, you will be reading, or chanting, Torah—in Hebrew. You will be reading, or chanting, the haftarah—in Hebrew. That is the major skill that publicly marks the becoming of bar or bat mitzvah. But, perhaps even more important than that, you need to be able to teach something about the Torah portion, and perhaps the haftarah as well.

And that is where this book comes in. It will be a very valuable resource for you, and your family, in the b'nai mitzvah process.

Here is what you will find in it:

> A brief **summary** of every Torah portion. This is a basic overview of the portion; and, while it might not refer to everything in the Torah portion, it will explain its most important aspects.
> A list of the **major ideas** in the Torah portion. The purpose: to make the Torah portion real, in ways that we can relate to. Every Torah portion contains unique ideas, and when you put all

of those ideas together, you actually come up with a list of Judaism's most important ideas.

> Two *divrei Torah* ("words of Torah," or "sermonettes") for each portion. These *divrei Torah* explain significant aspects of the Torah portion in accessible, reader-friendly language. Each *devar Torah* contains references to **traditional** Jewish sources (those that were written before the modern era), as well as **modern** sources and quotes. We have searched, far and wide, to find sources that are unusual, interesting, and not just the "same old stuff" that many people already know about the Torah portion. Why did we include these minisermons in the volume? Not because we want you to simply copy those sermons and pass them off as your own (that would be cheating), though you are free to quote from them. We included them so that you can see what is possible—how you can try to make meaning for yourself out of the words of Torah.

> **Connections:** This is perhaps the most valuable part. It's a list of questions that you can ask yourself, or that others might help you think about—any of which can lead to the creation of your *devar Torah*.

Note: you don't have to like everything that's in a particular Torah portion. Some aren't that loveable. Some are hard to understand; some are about religious practices that people today might find confusing, and even offensive; some contain ideas that we might find totally outmoded.

But this doesn't have to get in the way. After all, most kids spend a lot of time thinking about stories that contain ideas that modern people would find totally bizarre. Any good medieval fantasy story falls into that category.

And we also believe that, if you spend just a little bit of time with those texts, you can begin to understand what the author was trying to say.

This volume goes one step further. Sometimes, the haftarah comes off as a second thought, and no one really thinks about it. We have tried to solve that problem by including a **summary** of each haftarah, and then a mini-sermon on the haftarah. This will help you learn how these sacred words are relevant to today's world, and even to your own life.

All Bible quotations come from the NJPS translation, which is found in the many different editions of the JPS TANAKH; in the Conservative movement's *Etz Hayim: Torah and Commentary;* in the Reform movement's *Torah: A Modern Commentary;* and in other Bible commentaries and study guides.

How Do I Write a *Devar Torah?*

It really is easier than it looks.

There are many ways of thinking about the *devar Torah.* It is, of course, a short sermon on the meaning of the Torah (and, perhaps, the haftarah) portion. It might even be helpful to think of the *devar Torah* as a "book report" on the portion itself.

The most important thing you can know about this sacred task is: *Learn* the words. *Love* the words. Teach people what it could mean to *live* the words.

Here's a basic outline for a *devar Torah:*

"My Torah portion is (name of portion)_____,
   from the book of _____, chapter

_____.

"In my Torah portion, we learn that_____
   (Summary of portion)

"For me, the most important lesson of this Torah portion is (what is the best thing in the portion? Take the portion as a whole; your *devar Torah* does not have to be only, or specifically, on the verses that you are reading).

"As I learned my Torah portion, I found myself wondering:
  › *Raise a question that the Torah portion itself raises.*
  › *"Pick a fight"* with the portion. Argue with it.
  › *Answer a question* that is listed in the "Connections" section of each Torah portion.
  › *Suggest a question to your rabbi* that you would want the rabbi to answer in his or her own *devar Torah* or sermon.

"I have lived the values of the Torah by _____
(here, you can talk about how the Torah portion relates to your
own life. If you have done a mitzvah project, you can talk about
that here).

How To Keep It from Being Boring (and You from Being Bored)

Some people just don't like giving traditional speeches. From our per-
spective, that's really okay. Perhaps you can teach Torah in a different
way—one that makes sense to you.

> ➤ Write an "open letter" to one of the characters in your Torah por-
> tion. "Dear Abraham: I hope that your trip to Canaan was not too
> hard . . ." "Dear Moses: Were you afraid when you got the Ten
> Commandments on Mount Sinai? I sure would have been . . ."
> ➤ Write a news story about what happens. Imagine yourself to
> be a television or news reporter. "Residents of neighboring cit-
> ies were horrified yesterday as the wicked cities of Sodom and
> Gomorrah were burned to the ground. Some say that God was
> responsible . . ."
> ➤ Write an imaginary interview with a character in your Torah portion.
> ➤ Tell the story from the point of view of another character, or a mi-
> nor character, in the story. For instance, tell the story of the Gar-
> den of Eden from the point of view of the serpent. Or the story
> of the Binding of Isaac from the point of view of the ram, which
> was substituted for Isaac as a sacrifice. Or perhaps the story of
> the sale of Joseph from the point of view of his coat, which was
> stripped off him and dipped in a goat's blood.
> ➤ Write a poem about your Torah portion.
> ➤ Write a song about your Torah portion.
> ➤ Write a play about your Torah portion, and have some friends act
> it out with you.
> ➤ Create a piece of artwork about your Torah portion.

The bottom line is: Make this a joyful experience. Yes—it could
even be fun.

The Very Last Thing You Need to Know at This Point

The Torah scroll is written without vowels. Why? Don't *sofrim* (Torah scribes) know the vowels?

Of course they do.

So, why do they leave the vowels out?

One reason is that the Torah came into existence at a time when sages were still arguing about the proper vowels, and the proper pronunciation.

But here is another reason: The Torah text, as we have it today, and as it sits in the scroll, is actually *an unfinished work*. Think of it: the words are just sitting there. Because they have no vowels, it is as if they have no voice.

When we read the Torah publicly, we give voice to the ancient words. And when we find meaning in those ancient words, and we talk about those meanings, those words jump to life. They enter our lives. They make our world deeper and better.

Mazal tov to you, and your family. This is your journey toward Jewish maturity. Love it.

THE TORAH

❖ Be-ḥukkotai: Leviticus 26:3–27:34

Just in case you were looking forward to this, the last portion of Leviticus, you should know that it's a bit of a downer. Actually, make that a major downer. God tells the Israelites what will happen if they follow God's laws. That part is okay—but the part about what will happen if they don't obey God's laws—oy.

This parashah, and all of Leviticus, ends with a somewhat anticlimactic piece about the funding of the ancient sanctuary.

Summary

- God promises that if the Israelites observe God's commandments to observe the *shemitah* and the *yovel,* then God will bless the land with prosperity. (26:3–13)
- Big "but" coming: if the Israelites do not observe God's commandments, they are entering into a "world of pain." Illnesses, wild beasts, military defeat, the destruction of the Land of Israel—even cannibalism!—will follow. (26:14–45)
- God tells Moses details about the funding of the ancient Tabernacle—specific amounts people should give based on age and gender. There are also provisions for those who vow to donate animals that would be converted into money in support of the sanctuary, or who vow to donate land or tithe produce. (27:1–34)

The Big Ideas

> **Following God's commandments is a social good.** It's not that
> if you do God's will everything will be fine with you. It's not
> about "you"—in the singular. This passage tells us that if the Jew-
> ish people obey God, then good things will happen in their land.
> While this idea of reward and punishment is debatable (and
> many find it, frankly, ethically questionable, if not offensive), it is
> clearly what the biblical writers believed.

> **Actions have consequences.** If you are troubled by all the threat
> and punishment passages in Leviticus, join the club. It even has a
> name—the "reproof" (*tokhecha*). It is such a horrible section that
> in synagogue it is read quickly and in a low voice. You just want
> to get through it and get over it. But if you read the passage care-
> fully, you will notice that it is saying something important: societ-
> ies collapse when justice is not done.

> **It is a mitzvah to support the institutions of the Jewish com-
> munity.** Many people complain that "religion costs too much!" If
> that is true, then it has always been the case. The Torah specifies
> the amounts that people should give, based on age and gender, as
> well as other details of giving. These passages seem quite relevant
> to modern Jews, because people still argue about the best way to
> support synagogues and other Jewish institutions.

Divrei Torah

IS GOD A BULLY?

Bullies. Don't you hate them? But who ever expected that God would become The Supreme Bully? God seems to be threatening the Israelites with the ultimatum "Do what I say, or else . . ." Just read the list of curses that this Torah portion contains—everything from threatening to shut down the rain to (gulp) forcing the Israelites to "devour" their children.

Okay, let's figure this one out. Nachmanides, the medieval commentator, teaches: "You must know and understand that everything in this chapter actually took place during the First Temple period and its aftermath, including both the exile to Babylonia and the redemption from there, for that is when they worshiped idols and did all these evil things."

Then came the punishments, which seemed to be a fulfillment of the dire warnings of Leviticus. When the Assyrians destroyed the Northern Kingdom of Israel in 722 BCE, they did horrible things to the Jewish people and to the Land of Israel. The same sort of things happened two centuries later, when the Babylonians destroyed the Southern Kingdom of Judah.

Did God actually bring all those curses upon the Jewish people? Let's imagine it this way: perhaps the people were trying to figure out why all these terrible things had happened to them. In ancient times, the only real answer to that question would be: God. God was punishing the people for their sins. The Jews of ancient times believed that God "used" the enemies of the Jews as a way of disciplining God's people for their sins.

What were those sins? The list is long, and includes the sin of failing to let the land rest for one year out of every seven (*shemitah*). The Torah warns that if the people don't observe *shemitah* they will be expelled from the land, and they won't be permitted to return until the land has made up for all the missed *shemitah* years (26:34–35). What is so bad about not letting the land rest? Because it has to do with not exploiting the land—and also the most vulnerable people who work the land.

So, God gives the Jewish people laws that help to create a just society. That was the whole purpose of *shemitah* (sabbatical year) and yovel (jubilee year, returning the land to its original owner every fifty years). If you don't create a just society, then that society will crumble. You will have people who show only callousness to the poor. That society will wind up in ruins—and you are free to imagine that God, who feels *very* strongly about justice, will punish you.

Cantor Sarah Sager describes the mindset of the final portion of Leviticus: "It is both bribe and promise, exhortation and encouragement. The physical and ethical dimensions of God's creation are dependent upon each other, and we ignore that relationship at our peril."

If we don't create a just society, that society will fall apart.

If you look at the long sweep of human history, societies that ignored social justice did, in fact, crumble—think of medieval Spain, Nazi Germany, the former Soviet Union.

Sometimes God may seem like a bully. The same with our parents. But we need to try to get behind the threats of punishment to the real issue of how we behave. There is definitely more here than meets the eye.

SACRED MONEY

We have come full circle . . . and it's about money! Go back to the end of the book of Exodus, and you will see it: Exodus ended on the subject of "how do we pay for the Tabernacle?" And that's how Leviticus ends as well.

The Torah portion has already figured out what people are "worth" in terms of taxation. A man between the ages of twenty to sixty is worth fifty shekels; a woman of the same age, thirty shekels. Once a man hits the age of sixty, his "value" drops to fifteen shekels, and a woman's drops to ten. Yes, it's sexist and ageist. But we're talking about something from long ago, and that's the way it was back then. (Come to think of it: has it really changed that much? Even nowadays, women earn less than men, and there is rampant age discrimination in the workplace.)

What is the best way to financially support our religious institutions? It's a question that we still wrestle with. Every institution costs money to sustain, and the modern synagogue is no exception. Though most synagogues today expect their members to pay a specific sum, called membership dues, this isn't always the case. Synagogues have all kinds of ways of raising the money they need, including voluntary giving.

Some are experimenting with a "pay what you want" system. Rabbi Rick Jacobs, the president of the Union for Reform Judaism, has supported this new approach and said that voluntary pledging may positively change the way people view their synagogues: "The bond that holds the Jewish people to one another is not primarily and fundamentally a financial arrangement, and when we suggest that it might be, it undermines everything we stand for."

A voluntary pledge seems very different from the ancient model described in our Torah portion. There, what you have to pay is spelled out. In postbiblical times, and in medieval times, the community could force its members to pay community dues. Maimonides teaches: "People of the city can force each other to build a wall, doors, and bolt; and a synagogue, and to buy a Torah scroll, and the Prophets and the Writings for anyone in the community who wants to read."

In other words, there was general agreement—a communal covenant, if you will—that a community needs to be physically secure (cities in the Middle Ages were frequently walled in order to keep out enemies), as well as spiritually vibrant, by having a synagogue, a Torah scroll, and a full Bible that would be available for people to read.

When you think about it, support of the Jewish community and its institutions is entirely voluntary today, since nobody forces you to be a member of a synagogue and pay dues. The fact remains, however: synagogues require money to keep the lights on and to pay salaries. They depend on the goodwill of people who feel a sense of responsibility to support the Jewish community.

Yes, it's another expense, and money is often tight. But if we don't support our synagogue and Jewish community, who will?

Connections

> How do you feel about the list of blessings and curses? Do they make you afraid? Angry?

> The tradition says that the curses should be read in synagogue quickly and in a low voice. Do you agree with that tradition? Do you have any other suggestions for dealing with passages in the Torah that seem offensive or frightening?

> Do you agree that unjust societies are often destroyed, either from the outside or from the inside? Can you give some examples? How could those societies have saved themselves?

> What do you think is the best way to support synagogues? Dues? Donations? Giving whatever you can?

THE HAFTARAH

❖ Be-ḥukkotai: Jeremiah 16:19–17:14

When it comes to the ancient Israelites, sin can be deadly—literally. That's one of the central ideas of the Hebrew Bible, and the prophet Jeremiah hammers it home for us in this final haftarah of the book of Leviticus.

The Torah portion speaks of the sins that (ancient Israelites believed) were the reason why they might be exiled from their land. The horrific conditions of destruction and exile, described in the Torah portion, had become living realities when the Assyrians and the Babylonians destroyed, respectively, the Northern Kingdom of Israel and the Southern Kingdom of Judah.

Jeremiah, living in the time of the destruction of Judah, has his own take on why it is happening. To the sins of idolatry and of exploitation of the vulnerable, Jeremiah adds one more: the sin of failing to trust in God. Jeremiah believes, therefore, that some of our sins come not from what we actually do; they come from how we feel—from what is going on inside of us.

Actions, Not Feelings

Someday this will happen to you. You will know someone who is wealthy (maybe it will be you!), and that person decides she wants to give a lot of money to a particular project. Let's say that she decides to donate money for the construction of a building on a college campus, or to a project in Israel.

Good, right? But then someone gets up and says: "You know, this woman who wants to give the money—I know that she just wants the honor and respect that comes with giving all that money! It's all about her ego; she doesn't really care that much about this project."

How are you going to react to this? Sure—we would hope that the giver is sincere. But what if she isn't sincere? What if she really doesn't care that much about the project and really just wants her name on the outside of the building?

So, it's time to talk about our inner lives—the stuff that happens inside us.

First, let's get real—very few people give a whole lot of money to things that don't interest them.

Second, and what if they didn't really care that much? Is that our business? Are the inner intentions and feelings of people really that important?

Jeremiah and other prophets did care about what we think. They wanted us to be pure on the inside and the outside. But, to be honest, the weight of Jewish tradition is on our words and our actions, not on our thoughts.

Let's go to an interesting example of this from the great medieval sage Maimonides. He created a famous "ladder of *tzedakah*," in which he explained the best kinds of giving, ranked from highest to lowest. The highest level: "To support a fellow Jew by endowing him with a gift or loan, or entering into a partnership with him, or finding employment for him, in order to strengthen his hand until he need no longer be dependent upon others." Go through all those levels of *tzedakah,* and you will find that secret giving (where the giver and the recipient don't know each other) is way up there as well. The second to lowest step: "When one gives inadequately, but gives gladly and with a smile."

So, according to Maimonides, when it comes to helping people, our own emotions really don't count for that much. What matters most is the actual giving (even if you scowl)!

Jeremiah himself acknowledged that you can never really know what a person is thinking: "Most devious is the heart; it is perverse— who can fathom it? I the Lord probe the heart, search the mind—to repay every man according to his ways, with the proper fruit of his deeds (17:9–10).

We can never be sure of what's going on in other people's hearts; only God knows that. By the way, quite often we ourselves are not totally clear about our own motives for doing something. Do I want to be class president for my personal glory, or because it will look good on my college application, or because I really want to help my school? If you do a good job, does it really matter?

When President Jimmy Carter said famously that he had sinned because he had lusted after another woman in his heart, many Jews were unsure what all the fuss was about. It's not like the president had an affair (unlike many other politicians).

As Rabbi Leonid Feldman writes: "Only God truly understands our motives, and what we humans should focus on are the deeds and not the heart."

Jeremiah and the prophets urged us to have good thoughts on the inside so we have good actions on the outside. But if you can't have both (and we are only human), focus not on the first, but on the second.

❖ Notes

CPSIA information can be obtained
at www.ICGtesting.com
Printed in the USA
LVHW091625011218
598911LV00001B/64/P